TREATS

just great recipes

GENERAL INFORMATION

The level of difficulty of the recipes in this book
is expressed as a number from 1 (simple) to 3 (difficult).

TREATS
just great recipes
filled pasta

McRae Books

Making Filled Pasta

Many of the recipes in this book can be made using filled pasta bought from a specialty store or supermarket. However, we have also included instructions so that you can make them at home.

SERVES 4

PREPARATION 30 min + 30 min to rest

DIFFICULTY level 2

Fresh Pasta

Plain Pasta
3 cups (450 g) all-purpose (plain) flour
4 large eggs

Spinach or Tomato Pasta
2½ cups (375 g) all-purpose (plain) flour
3 large eggs
2 oz (60 g) spinach purée or tomato paste

Whole-Wheat (Wholemeal) Pasta
2 cups (300 g) all-purpose (plain)
   flour
1 cups (150 g) whole-wheat
   (wholemeal) flour
4 large eggs

1 Sift the flour and salt into a mound on a clean work surface. Make a hollow in the center and break the eggs into it one by one. Using a fork, gradually mix the eggs into the flour. If making spinach or tomato pasta, add the spinach purée or tomato paste now. Continue until all the flour has been incorporated.

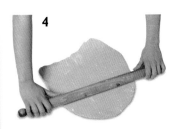

2 At a certain point the dough will be too thick to mix with a fork. Use your hands to shape it into a ball. It should be smooth and not sticky.

3 Knead the dough by pushing downward and forward on the ball of pasta with the heel of your palm. Fold the dough in half, give it a quarter-turn, and repeat the process. Knead for 15–20 minutes. Set the kneaded dough aside for 30 minutes to rest.

4 To roll the pasta by hand, flour a clean work surface and place a rolling pin on the top of the ball. Push outward from the center. When the dough is about ¼ inch (5 mm) thick, curl the far edge of the dough around the pin and gently stretch it as you roll it onto the pin. Unroll and repeat until the dough is almost transparent.

5 To roll the dough using a pasta machine, divide it into 4–6 pieces and flatten by hand. Set the machine with its rollers at the widest and run each piece through. Reduce the width by a notch and repeat until all the pasta has been rolled at the thinnest setting. Cut into sheets about 12 inches (30 cm) long. Attach the cutters to the pasta machine and set it at the widths given for the various types of pasta. Lay the cut pasta out on clean cloths to dry for 2 hours before use.

Making Filled Pasta

TO MAKE AGNOLOTTI, RAVIOLI, OR TORTELLI

TO MAKE TORTELLINI

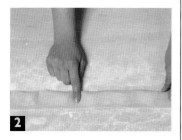

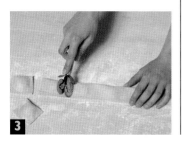

Agnolotti, Ravioli, Tortelli:

1 Cut the rolled dough into sheets 4 inches (10 cm) wide. Place teaspoons of filling at intervals of 2 inches (5 cm) down the center.

2 Moisten the edges of the dough with a little water and fold it over to seal. Press down lightly between the mounds of filling.

3 Use a sharp knife or fluted pastry cutter to cut between the mounds. If using a wheel cutter, roll it around the other sides so that they are attractively fluted too. Lay the stuffed pasta out on clean cloths for 2 hours before use.

4 **Tortellini:** Cut the rolled dough into sheets about 2 inches (5 cm) wide. Cut them in squares.

5 Place teaspoonfuls of the filling mixture at the center of each. Moisten the edges of the pasta with a little water and fold over into a triangular shape.

6 Fold the top of the triangle over and pull the edges around to meet. Pinch the edges together and seal them. Lay the stuffed pasta out on clean cloths for 2 hours before cooking.

Sausage Ravioli

with butter and sage sauce

Prepare the pasta dough and set aside to rest. • Cook the spinach and chard in a pot of salted water for 8–10 minutes, or until tender. Squeeze out excess moisture and chop finely. • Mix the sausages, ricotta, eggs, half the Parmesan, and the marjoram with the spinach and chard in a bowl. Combine thoroughly and season with salt. • Roll out the pasta and prepare the ravioli as shown on page 5. • Cook in a large pot of salted boiling water until al dente, 3–4 minutes. • While the ravioli are cooking, prepare the sauce: Melt the butter in a small saucepan over low heat. Add the sage leaves and simmer until the butter is just pale gold, 2–3 minutes. • Drain the ravioli and place in a heated serving dish. Pour the sauce over the top and sprinkle with the remaining Parmesan. Serve hot.

1 quantity Plain Pasta dough (see page 4)

8 oz (250 g) fresh spinach

1 lb (500 g) fresh Swiss chard (silver beet)

8 oz (250 g) Italian pork sausages, skinned and crumbled

8 oz (250 g) fresh ricotta cheese

2 large eggs

½ cup (60 g) freshly grated Parmesan cheese

1 teaspoon finely chopped fresh marjoram

Salt

½ cup (125 g) butter

8–10 fresh sages leaves

SERVES 4
PREPARATION 30 min + time for pasta and sauce
COOKING 35 min
DIFFICULTY level 3

Potato Tortelli
with meat sauce

Prepare the meat sauce. • Prepare the pasta dough and set aside to rest. • Cook the potatoes in a pot of salted, boiling water for 25 minutes, or until tender. Drain, slip off their skins, and mash. Place in a large bowl with the egg, half the Parmesan, the butter, nutmeg, salt, and pepper. Mix well. • Roll out the pasta and prepare the tortelli as shown on page 5. • Cook the tortelli in a large pot of salted boiling water until al dente, 3–4 minutes. Drain and place in a heated serving dish. Pour the meat sauce over the top. Sprinkle with the remaining Parmesan and serve hot.

1 quantity Meat Sauce
(see recipe, page 32)

1 quantity Plain Pasta dough
(see page 4)

1½ lb (750 g) potatoes
1 large fresh egg
1 cup (120 g) freshly grated Parmesan cheese
2 tablespoons butter
Pinch of nutmeg
Salt and freshly ground black pepper

SERVES 4–6

PREPARATION 30 min + time for pasta

COOKING 1 h

DIFFICULTY level 3

Spinach Ravioli
with tomato sauce

Prepare the spinach pasta dough and set aside to rest. • Tomato Sauce: Sauté the garlic in ¼ cup (60 ml) of oil in a large saucepan over medium heat until pale gold, 2–3 minutes. • Add the oregano, marjoram, basil, and tomatoes. Mix in the sun-dried tomatoes and season with salt and pepper. • Partially cover and simmer for 45 minutes over low heat, stirring occasionally. • Place the ricotta in a bowl. Add the parsley, basil, eggs, nutmeg, and salt. Mix well. • Roll out the pasta and prepare the ravioli as shown on page 5. • Cook the ravioli in a large pot of salted boiling water until al dente, 3–4 minutes. Drain well and place in a heated serving dish. • Pour the tomato sauce over the ravioli and toss carefully. Sprinkle with the Parmesan and serve hot.

1 quantity Spinach Pasta dough (see page 4)

Tomato Sauce

4–5 cloves garlic, finely chopped

⅓ cup (90 ml) extra-virgin olive oil

2 tablespoons finely chopped oregano

1 tablespoon finely chopped marjoram

1 tablespoon finely chopped basil

2 lb (1 kg) tomatoes, peeled and chopped

2 oz (60 g) sun-dried tomatoes, finely chopped

Salt and freshly ground black pepper

Ravioli

1 cup (250 g) fresh ricotta, drained

4 cups parsley and 5 cups fresh basil, finely chopped

2 large eggs

¼ teaspoon nutmeg

Salt

¼ cup (30 g) freshly grated Parmesan cheese

Ravioli

with beef and spinach filling

Prepare the pasta dough and set aside to rest. • Filling: Sauté the onion in 3 tablespoons og butter in a large frying pan over medium heat until softened, about 5 minutes. • Add the veal and cook until browned all over, about 8 minutes. • Season with salt and add the water. • Cover and simmer over low heat for 90 minutes. • Transfer to a cutting board and coarsely chop. • Sauté the spinach and Swiss chard in the remaining 3 tablespoons butter in a separate frying pan over high heat for 3 minutes. Sprinkle with parsley and basil. Remove from the heat, and add the chopped meat. • Mix in the egg and season with salt and pepper. • Roll out the pasta and prepare the ravioli as shown on page 5. • Cook the pasta in small batches in a large pot of salted boiling water until al dente, 3–4 minutes. • Drain and drizzle with the cooking juices and butter. Sprinkle with Parmesan and serve.

1 quantity Plain Pasta Dough
(see page 4)

Filling

1 onion, finely chopped

1/3 cup (90 g) butter

12 oz (350 g) lean veal or beef,
cut into small chunks

Salt

1 tablespoon water

2 cups (200 g) cooked spinach, drained

3/4 cup (100 g) cooked Swiss chard,
drained

1 tablespoon finely chopped fresh
parsley

6 leaves fresh basil, torn

1 large egg, lightly beaten

Freshly ground black pepper

Cooking juices from roast meat

2 tablespoons butter, melted

2 tablespoons freshly grated Parmesan
cheese

Agnolotti
with spinach and meat filling

Filling: Marinate the beef and pork in a large bowl with the onion, carrot, celery, garlic, cloves, peppercorns, salt, oil, and wine. Chill for 12 hours. • Transfer the marinated meat and vegetables with the liquid to a large deep frying pan. Add the pancetta, cover, and simmer over low heat for 4 hours, until the meat is tender, adding stock or water as required. • Prepare the pasta dough and set aside to rest. • Cook the rice in the milk over medium heat until tender, 15–20 minutes. Season with salt. Drain well. • Chop the meat in a food processor until finely ground. • Transfer to a bowl and mix in the rice, spinach, Parmesan, and eggs. Season with salt and nutmeg. • Roll out the pasta and prepare the agnolotti as shown on page 5. • Cook the pasta in small batches in a large pot of salted boiling water until al dente, 3–4 minutes. • Drain well and drizzle with the melted butter and the sage. Sprinkle with Parmesan and serve.

Filling
8 oz (250 g) lean beef, chopped
4 oz (150 g) lean pork, chopped
1/2 onion, thinly sliced
1 carrot, cut into rounds
1 stalk celery, chopped
1 clove garlic, lightly crushed but whole
2 cloves
5 black peppercorns
Salt
3 tablespoons extra-virgin olive oil
1 1/3 cups (300 ml) dry red wine
2 oz (60 g) pancetta, sliced
1/4 cup (60 ml) beef stock or water
   (optional)
1/4 cup (50 g) long-grain rice
2/3 cup (150 ml) milk
2 cups (200 g) cooked spinach, drained
2 tablespoons freshly grated Parmesan
   cheese
2 large eggs
1/2 teaspoon nutmeg

1 quantity Plain Pasta Dough
   (see page 4)

2/3 cup (150 g) butter, melted
2 small bunches fresh sage
1/2 cup (60 g) freshly grated Parmesan
   cheese

SERVES 4–6

PREPARATION 1 h + 1 h to rest
+ time for pasta

COOKING 1 h

DIFFICULTY level 3

Tortelli

with sweet squash filling

Prepare the pasta dough and set aside to rest. • Preheat the oven to 400°F (200°C/gas 6). • Bake the pieces of squash on a large baking sheet for 40–45 minutes, or until tender. • Remove from the oven and let cool. Use a tablespoon to remove the flesh from the peel and purée in a food processor. If the squash is still moist, wrap it in a muslin cloth and wring out the excess moisture. • Filling: Transfer the squash purée to a large bowl and mix in the amaretti, eggs, Parmesan, Mostarda di Cremona, and nutmeg. Season with salt. If the mixture seems coarse, process until smooth. • Let rest for at least 1 hour at room temperature or overnight in the refrigerator. • Roll out the pasta and prepare the tortelli as shown on page 5. • Cook in small batches in a large pot of salted boiling water until al dente, 3–4 minutes. • Drain well. Transfer to a serving dish and drizzle with the melted butter.

1 quantity Plain Pasta Dough
(see page 4)

Filling
2 lb (1 kg) winter squash (pumpkin), unpeeled, cut into large pieces and seeded
³⁄₄ cup (100 g) amaretti cookies, very finely crushed
2 large eggs
³⁄₄ cup (90 g) freshly grated Parmesan cheese
¹⁄₂ cup (100 g) mostarda di Cremona or fruit chutney, finely chopped
¹⁄₈ teaspoon freshly grated nutmeg
Salt
¹⁄₃ cup (90 g) butter, melted

Folded Agnolotti

Prepare the pasta dough and set aside to rest. • Filling: Cook the cabbage and lettuce in salted boiling water until wilted, about 5 minutes. • Drain, chop finely, and set aside. • Braise the veal in 2 tablespoons of butter with the onion, bay leaf, and celery over medium heat until the meat is tender, gradually adding all the stock as the meat begins to dry. • Discard the onion, bay leaf, and celery and chop the veal in a food processor until finely ground. • Sauté the garlic, rosemary, and parsley in the remaining 2 tablespoons of butter and oil in a large frying pan over medium heat until the garlic is pale gold, 2–3 minutes. • Add the ground meat and sauté over high heat until browned all over, about 5 minutes. • Add the cabbage and lettuce and simmer for 3 minutes. • Remove from the heat and let cool to warm. • Mix in the egg and half the Parmesan and season with salt, pepper, and nutmeg. • Roll out the dough on a lightly floured surface until paper-thin. Cut into 4½-inch (10-cm) wide strips and arrange small heaps of filling near one edge, about ¾ inch (3 cm) apart. • Fold each strip of dough lengthwise to cover the filling. Seal, after making sure no air pockets remain, then cut into squares with a ravioli cutter. Pinch as it you were going to fold it in half. • Cook the pasta in small batches in a large pot of salted boiling water until al dente, 3–4 minutes. • Use a slotted spoon to transfer to a serving dish and drizzle with butter. Sprinkle with marjoram and Parmesan and serve hot.

1 quantity Plain Pasta Dough
(see page 4)

Filling
8 oz (200 g) Savoy cabbage
1 head butterhead lettuce
1 lb (500 g) veal or beef,
in a single cut
¼ cup (60 g) butter
½ onion
1 bay leaf
1 stalk celery
2 cups (500 ml) meat stock or broth
2 cloves garlic, finely chopped
1 sprig fresh rosemary
1 sprig fresh parsley, finely chopped
2 tablespoons extra-virgin olive oil
1 large egg
1 cup (120 g) freshly grated Parmesan
cheese
Salt and freshly ground black pepper
½ teaspoon freshly grated nutmeg
½ cup (125 g) butter, melted
3 sprigs fresh marjoram, finely chopped

SERVES 4–6

PREPARATION 30 min + time for pasta

COOKING 20 min

DIFFICULTY level 3

Beet Tortelli

Prepare the pasta dough and set aside to rest. • Filling: Chop the beets and sauté over high heat in $^1/_3$ cup (90 g) of butter and a dash of salt. • Remove from the heat, stir in the ricotta, adding some bread crumbs if the filling is too moist. • Roll out the pasta dough to a thin, almost transparent sheet. • Use the rim of a 3-inch (8-cm) glass or round cookie cutter to cut out disks. • Place a little of the filling in the center of each disk and fold it in half, enclosing the filling. Pinch the edges firmly together with the tips of your fingers to seal. • Cook the pasta in batches in a large pot of salted boiling water until al dente, 3–4 minutes. • Use a slotted spoon to transfer the tortelli to serving dishes. Dot with the remaining butter and sprinkle with the poppy seeds. • Serve hot.

1 quantity Plain Pasta Dough (see page 4)

Filling
2 lb (1 kg) boiled beets (beet root)
$^3/_4$ cup (180 g) butter
Salt
$^1/_2$ cup (125 g) ricotta cheese, drained
fine bread crumbs (to be used if needed)
4 tablespoons poppy seeds

Seafood Ravioli

Prepare the pasta dough and set aside to rest. • Filling: Fill a medium saucepan with cold water and add the onion, pepper, bay leaf, and parsley. Season with salt, bring to a boil, and simmer for 20 minutes. • Add the hake and cook over low heat for 5 minutes. • Drain the hake, remove the skin and bones, and chop finely • Heat 1 tablespoon of garlic-flavored oil in a large frying pan. Add the white fish and sauté over high heat for 2 minutes. Pour in the sherry and let it evaporate. Remove from heat and finely chop. • Lightly flour the scallops. Melt the butter in a small frying pan and sauté the scallops until tender, 3–4 minutes. Season with salt and chop finely. • Mix the hake, white fish, and scallops in a medium bowl. Season with salt and pepper and add 1 tablespoon of garlic-flavored oil. Stir in the egg and parsley. • Roll out the pasta and prepare the ravioli as shown on page 5. • Sauce: Heat the remaining garlic-flavored oil in a large frying pan and add the white fish and shrimp. Sauté for 2 minutes over high heat. Add the vermouth and let it evaporate. Set the fish aside. • Add the tomatoes to the same pan. Season with salt and pepper. Simmer for 5–10 minutes over low heat. • Cook the pasta in batches in a large pot of salted boiling water until al dente, 3–4 minutes. • Use a slotted spoon to transfer to the pan with the tomatoes. Add the fish mixture and the butter and toss gently. • Serve hot.

1 quantity Plain Pasta Dough
  (see page 4)

Filling
½ white onion
1 bay leaf
3 grains pepper
2 sprigs parsley
Salt and freshly ground black pepper
8 oz (250 g) hake, chopped
2 cloves garlic, soaked in ¼ cup
  (60 ml) extra-virgin olive oil
12 oz (350 g) white fish fillets,
  chopped
2 tablespoons sherry
4 tablespoons all-purpose (plain) flour
8 oz (250 g) shelled scallops, diced
2 tablespoons butter
1 egg
1 tablespoon finely chopped fresh
  parsley

Sauce
8 oz (250 g) shelled shrimp, chopped
8 oz (250 g) white fish fillets
12 oz (350 g) peeled and chopped
  tomatoes
2 tablespoons vermouth
2 tablespoons butter

Tortelli

with amaretti and spice

Prepare the pasta dough and set aside to rest. • Filling: Toast the bread crumbs in 2 tablespoons of the butter in a medium frying pan over medium heat until browned, about 5 minutes. • Transfer to a bowl with the amaretti cookies, 1¼ cups (150 g) of Parmesan, raisins, candied lemon peel, egg, and spices. Season with salt and pepper. If the mixture is dry and crumbly, add the stock. • Roll out the pasta and prepare the tortelli as shown on page 5. • Cook the pasta in a large pot of salted boiling water until al dente, 3–4 minutes. • Remove with a slotted spoon and transfer to a serving dish. Drizzle with the remaining ⅔ cup (150 g) melted butter and sprinkle with the remaining Parmesan. Serve hot.

1 quantity Plain Pasta Dough
(see page 4)

Filling

3 tablespoons fresh bread crumbs

2 tablespoons butter, cut up
+ ⅔ cup (150 g), melted

1¼ cups (150 g) crushed amaretti cookies

1¾ cups (210 g) freshly grated Parmesan cheese

¼ cup (50 g) golden raisins (sultanas)

½ cup (50 g) finely chopped candied lemon peel

1 large egg

1 teaspoon ground allspice (cinnamon, cloves and nutmeg in equal quantities)

Salt and freshly ground white pepper

1–2 tablespoons vegetable stock

SERVES 6–8

PREPARATION 2 h

COOKING 45 min

DIFFICULTY level 3

Tortelli
with chestnuts

Pasta Dough: Sift the all-purpose and chestnut flours and salt onto a surface and make a well in the center. Break the eggs into the well and mix in with enough water to make a smooth dough. Knead for 15–20 minutes, until smooth and elastic. Shape the dough into a ball, wrap in plastic wrap (cling film), and let rest for 30 minutes. • Filling: Slice the chestnuts in half and cook in boiling water for 10 minutes. • Drain and strip them of their internal and external peels. Transfer to a large saucepan and add enough water to cover completely. Season with salt and add the bay leaf. • Bring to a boil and cook until tender, 35–45 minutes. Drain. • Mash the chestnuts and add the ricotta, eggs, and ¾ cup (90 g) of Parmesan. Season with salt and pepper. • Roll out the pasta and prepare the tortelli as shown on page 5. • Cook the pasta in a large pot of salted boiling water until al dente, 3–5 minutes. • Drain well and transfer to serving plates. Drizzle with the butter and sprinkle with the remaining Parmesan.

Pasta Dough
2⅓ cups (350 g) all-purpose (plain) flour
1 cup (150 g) chestnut flour
¼ teaspoon salt
3 large eggs
8–10 tablespoons warm water

Filling
1½ lb (750 g) chestnuts
Salt
1 bay leaf
Generous ¾ cup (200 g) ricotta cheese
2 large eggs
1½ cups (180 g) freshly grated Parmesan cheese
Salt and freshly ground black pepper
½ cup (125 g) butter, melted

SERVES 6

PREPARATION 1 h + time for pasta

COOKING 60 min

DIFFICULTY level 3

Ravioli
with cabbage and rice filling

Prepare the pasta dough and set aside to rest. • Filling: Cook the rice in salted boiling water until just tender, 12–15 minutes. • Cook the cabbage in a large saucepan of salted boiling water until tender, 5–7 minutes. Drain well, squeeze dry, and chop finely. • Sauté the onion in the butter in a large frying pan over medium heat until lightly browned, about 5 minutes. Season with salt. Simmer over low heat for 15 minutes. • Add the cabbage and simmer for 5 minutes. • Add the garlic and rice and season with salt and pepper. • Remove from the heat and transfer to a large bowl. Mix in the Parmesan and egg and let cool to lukewarm. • Roll out the pasta and prepare the ravioli as shown on page 5. • Cook the pasta in small batches in a large pot of salted boiling water until al dente, 3–4 minutes. • Use a slotted spoon to transfer to a serving dish and drizzle with butter. Sprinkle with Parmesan and serve.

1 quantity Plain Pasta Dough
(see page 4)

Filling
$1/2$ cup (100 g) long-grain rice
1 small Savoy cabbage, finely shredded
1 onion, finely chopped
3 tablespoons butter
Salt and freshly ground white pepper
2 cloves garlic, finely chopped
5 tablespoons freshly grated Parmesan
cheese
1 large egg

To serve
$1/2$ cup (125 g) butter, melted
1 cup (125 g) freshly grated Parmesan
cheese

SERVES 4–6

PREPARATION 45 min + time for pasta

COOKING 30 min

DIFFICULTY level 3

Arugula Ravioli
with pesto

Prepare the pasta dough and set aside to rest. • Boil the Swiss chard and arugula in salted water until tender, about 5 minutes. • Drain well, squeeze out excess moisture, and chop finely. • Place in a bowl and stir in the ricotta, Parmesan, and egg yolks. Season with salt and pepper and refrigerate until ready to use. • Roll out the pasta dough into a thin, almost transparent sheet. • Use a glass or cookie cutter to cut the pasta into 2-inch (5-cm) disks. • Place 1 teaspoon of filling at the center of half of the disks and cover each one with another disk of pasta. Press down on the edges to seal. • Cook the pasta in batches in a large pot of salted boiling water until al dente, 3–4 minutes. • Mix the pesto with 2 tablespoons of cooking water. • Use a slotted spoon to transfer the ravioli to a heated serving dish. Spoon the pesto over the top. • Serve hot.

1 quantity Plain Pasta Dough (see page 4)

1¼ lb (600 g) Swiss chard (silverbeet), stalks removed
10 oz (300 g) arugula (rocket)
½ cup (125 g) ricotta cheese, drained
6 tablespoons freshly grated Parmesan cheese
2 large egg yolks
Salt and freshly ground white pepper
1 quantity Pesto (see page 44)

SERVES 4–6

PREPARATION 30 min + time for pasta

COOKING 15 min

DIFFICULTY level 3

Cheese Ravioli

with butter and peppercorns

Prepare the pasta dough and set aside to rest. • Place the soft white cheese in a medium bowl and mix in the ricotta, Parmesan, eggs, salt, and pepper to make a smooth cream. Refrigerate until ready to use. • Roll out the pasta dough into a thin, almost transparent sheet. • Cut the dough into disks about 3 inches (8 cm) in diameter. • Place a heaped tablespoon of filling in the center of half of the disks of pasta. Cover each filled disk with another disk of pasta, pressing down on the edges to seal. • If liked, cut around the edges of the ravioli with a fluted pastry cutter. • Cook the pasta in batches in a large pot of salted boiling water until al dente, 3–4 minutes. • Use a slotted spoon to transfer to serving dishes. • Melt the butter in a small saucepan and sauté the peppercorns for 1–2 minutes. • Drizzle the butter and peppercorns over the ravioli and serve hot.

1 quantity Plain Pasta Dough (see page 4)

8 oz (250 g) soft fresh white cheese, such as mascarpone

$^2/_3$ cup (150 g) ricotta cheese

1 cup (125 g) freshly grated Parmesan cheese

2 large eggs

Salt and freshly ground white pepper

$^1/_3$ cup (90 g) butter

4 tablespoons green peppercorns, pickled in vinegar

SERVES 4–6

PREPARATION 15 min + 30 min to rest

COOKING 15 min

DIFFICULTY level 1

Ravioli
with walnut pesto and tomatoes

Chop the walnuts, garlic, marjoram, coarse salt, and Parmesan in a food processor. Add the oil, water, and bread crumbs and chop until smooth. • Transfer to a large bowl, cover with plastic wrap (cling film), and set aside to rest for 30 minutes. • Cook the pasta in small batches in a large pot of salted boiling water until al dente, 3–4 minutes. • Use a slotted spoon to transfer to serving dishes. • Cut the tomatoes in half and add to the sauce in the bowl. • Pour the sauce over the pasta and toss gently. • Season generously with black pepper and serve hot.

- 1 cup (150 g) shelled walnuts
- 2 cloves garlic
- 1 small bunch fresh marjoram
- 1 teaspoon coarse sea salt
- ⅔ cup (75 g) freshly grated Parmesan cheese
- ⅓ cup (90 ml) extra-virgin olive oil
- 1 tablespoon warm water
- 1½ cups (90 g) fresh bread crumbs soaked in ¼ cup (60 ml) milk
- 1 lb (500 g) storebought ravioli with spinach filling
- 16–20 cherry tomatoes
- Freshly ground black pepper

SERVES 6

PREPARATION 50 min + time for pasta

COOKING 45–50 min

DIFFICULTY level 3

Plaited Tortelli
with potato and mortadella

Prepare the pasta dough and set aside to rest. • Filling: Cook the potatoes in salted boiling water until tender 10–15 minutes. • Drain well and mash until smooth. • Melt the 2 tablespoons of butter in a large frying pan. Add the onion and sauté over medium heat until softened, about 5 minutes. • Increase the heat and add the spinach. Sauté for 2 minutes and season with salt and pepper. • Transfer the spinach mixture, mortadella, parsley, ½ cup (60 g) of Parmesan, bread crumbs, and egg to a food processor and process until smooth. • Roll out the dough until very thin on a floured work surface. Cut into 4-inch (10-cm) disks and drop a generous teaspoon of the filling onto the center of each one. Fold one flap of dough over the filling. Continue folding over flaps of dough, alternating from right to left, until you have completely enclosed the filling. • Cook the pasta in small batches in a large pot of salted boiling water until al dente, 3–4 minutes. • Use a slotted spoon to transfer to a serving dish and drizzle with the melted butter. Sprinkle with the remaining Parmesan and serve hot.

1 quantity Plain Pasta Dough
  (see page 4)

Filling and Topping
2 boiling potatoes, peeled and diced
½ cup (125 g) butter, melted
  + 2 tablespoons, cut up
1 small onion, finely chopped
1 cup (150 g) finely chopped cooked
  spinach
Salt and freshly ground white pepper
¾ cup (90 g) diced mortadella
1 sprig fresh parsley, finely chopped
1 cup (125 g) freshly grated Parmesan
  cheese
3 tablespoons fine dry bread crumbs
1 large egg

Ricotta Ravioli
with meat sauce

Prepare the pasta dough and set aside to rest. • Sauce: Use a meat pounder to tenderize the beef until flattened. • Sprinkle with pecorino, garlic, red pepper flakes, and parsley. Roll the meat up and tie with kitchen string. • Sauté the pancetta in the oil in a large frying pan over medium heat until crisp, about 5 minutes. • Carefully place the roll of beef in the pan and simmer over high heat for about 5 minutes. • Pour in the wine and let it evaporate. • Stir in the tomatoes, season with salt and pepper, and add the basil. Cover and simmer until the meat is tender, about 2 hours. Serve the meat as a main course. Filling: Mix the ricotta, eggs, pecorino, parsley, salt and pepper in a large bowl. Chill for 30 minutes. • Roll out the pasta and prepare the ravioli as shown on page 5. • Cook the pasta in batches in a large pot of salted boiling water until al dente, 3–4 minutes. • Top with the sauce.

1 quantity Plain Pasta Dough
(see page 4)

Sauce
1 lb (500 g) beef or pork,
in a single cut
3 tablespoons freshly grated pecorino
cheese
1 clove garlic, finely chopped
$\frac{1}{8}$ teaspoon red pepper flakes
1 tablespoon finely chopped fresh
parsley
2 slices of pancetta or bacon, cut into
short lengths
$\frac{1}{4}$ cup (60 ml) extra-virgin olive oil
$\frac{1}{3}$ cup (90 ml) dry white wine
1 lb (500 g) peeled plum tomatoes,
pressed through a fine mesh
strainer (passata)
Salt and freshly ground black pepper
Leaves from 1 small bunch fresh basil,
torn

Filling
1$\frac{1}{2}$ cups (400 g) ricotta, drained
2 large eggs
$\frac{1}{2}$ cup (60 g) freshly grated pecorino
cheese
2 tablespoons finely chopped fresh
parsley

SERVES 4–6

PREPARATION 10 min

COOKING 1 h

DIFFICULTY level 1

Tortellini
with meat sauce

Sauté the onion, carrot, and celery in the butter in a large heavy-bottomed saucepan for 5–7 minutes. • Add the pork, beef, and chicken livers, moisten with half the wine and simmer until it has evaporated. • Stir in the tomatoes and remaining wine and season with salt and pepper. • Cover and leave to simmer gently for at least 1 hour. • Cook the pasta in a large pan of salted boiling water until al dente, 3–4 minutes. • Drain well and transfer to a heated serving dish. Spoon the sauce over the top and toss gently. • Serve hot.

1 onion, finely chopped

1 carrot, finely chopped

1 stalk celery, finely chopped

2 tablespoons butter

8 oz (250 g) ground (minced) lean pork

8 oz (250 g) ground (minced) lean beef

2 chicken livers, coarsely chopped

1 cup (250 ml) dry red wine

1 (14-oz/400-g) can tomatoes, with juice

Salt and freshly ground black pepper

1 lb (500 g) fresh, storebought tortellini

Mixed Tortellini

Prepare both pasta doughs and set aside to rest. • Filling: Mix the Parmesan, bread crumbs, egg, butter, nutmeg, salt, and pepper in a small bowl. Transfer to a piping bag and refrigerate until ready to use. • Divide each piece of pasta into 2 pieces. • Roll each piece out into a thin, almost transparent sheet. • Cut the dough into 1-inch (2.5-cm) squares. • Pipe marble-sized blobs of filling onto the center of each square and shape into tortellini following the instructions on page 5. Place on a floured cloth until ready to cook. • Sauce: Heat the butter in a medium saucepan and add the spinach. Simmer for 2–3 minutes. • Add the flour and simmer for 2–3 minutes. Add the stock, salt, and pepper. Bring to a boil and simmer over low heat for 15 minutes, stirring often. • Remove from the heat and chop finely in a food processor. Reheat then spoon most of it into individual serving dishes. • Cook the pasta in a large pot of salted, boiling water for 2 minutes. • Use a slotted spoon to transfer to the serving dishes on top of the sauce. Spoon the remaining sauce over the top. • Serve hot.

¹⁄₄ quantity Plain Pasta Dough (see page 4)
¹⁄₄ quantity Tomato Pasta Dough (see page 4)

Filling
12 tablespoons freshly grated Parmesan cheese
8 tablespoons fine dry bread crumbs
1 large egg
1¹⁄₂ tablespoons butter
Pinch of freshly grated nutmeg
Salt and freshly ground white pepper

Sauce
2 tablespoons butter
8 oz (250 g) cooked spinach, finely chopped
4 tablespoons all-purpose (plain) flour
2¹⁄₂ cups (600 ml) chicken stock
Salt and freshly ground white pepper

SERVES 4–6
PREPARATION 30 min + time for pasta
and sauce
COOKING 30 min
DIFFICULTY level 3

Ricotta Ravioli
with tomato sauce

Prepare the pasta dough and set aside to rest. • Filling: Mix the ricotta, eggs, sugar, parsley, lemon zest, nutmeg, cinnamon, salt, and pepper in a large bowl. • Roll out the pasta and prepare the ravioli as shown on page 5. • Cook the pasta in batches in a large pot of salted boiling water until al dente, 3–4 minutes. • Use a slotted spoon to transfer to serving dishes. Spoon the sauce over the top and sprinkle with the Parmesan. Garnish with the basil. Serve hot.

1 quantity Plain Pasta Dough
  (see page 4)

Filling
1 2/3 cups (400 g) ricotta, drained
2 large eggs
2 tablespoons sugar
1 tablespoon finely chopped fresh
  parsley
Finely grated zest of 1/2 lemon
1/8 teaspoon freshly grated nutmeg
1/4 teaspoon ground cinnamon
Salt and freshly ground white pepper

1 quantity Tomato Sauce (see page 8)
1 cup (125 g) freshly grated Parmesan
  cheese
Fresh basil, to garnish

SERVES 4–6

PREPARATION 30 min + time for pasta

COOKING 1 h

DIFFICULTY level 3

Squash Ravioli
with raisin and sherry sauce

Prepare the pasta dough and set aside to rest. • Filling: Preheat the oven to 350°F (180°C/gas 4). • Bake the squash for about 45 minutes, or until tender. • Place the squash in a large bowl and mash with a fork. • Add the onion, walnuts, and sage and season with salt and pepper. • Roll out the pasta and prepare the ravioli as shown on page 5. • Sauce: Melt the butter in a small frying pan. Add the shallot and sauté for 3 minutes. • Sprinkle with the flour. Stir in the stock and sherry and simmer for 1 minute. • Add the raisins and cook for 3 more minutes. Season with salt and pepper. • Cook the pasta in batches in a large pot of salted boiling water until al dente, 3–4 minutes. • Use a slotted spoon to transfer to serving dishes. • Drizzle with the sherry and raisin sauce. Serve hot.

1 quantity Plain Pasta Dough
(see page 4)

Filling
1 lb (500 g) winter squash (pumpkin),
peeled and thickly sliced
1/2 white onion, finely chopped
1/2 cup (60 g) finely chopped walnuts
1 tablespoon finely chopped fresh sage
Salt and freshly ground white pepper

Sauce
2 tablespoons butter
1 shallot, finely chopped
2 tablespoons all-purpose (plain) flour
1 cup (250 ml) beef stock
1/4 cup (60 ml) sweet sherry
1/2 cup (100 g) raisins

Asparagus Tortelli

Prepare the pasta dough and set aside to rest. • Filling: Cook the asparagus in salted boiling water until tender. • Set aside a few tips to garnish the finished dish. Transfer the remaining asparagus to a food processor and chop until smooth. • Cook the potatoes in their skins in salted, boiling water until tender, 15–20 minutes. Drain and slip off the skins. Mash while still hot. • Add the garlic, butter, asparagus cream, and onion seeds. Season with salt and pepper. • Prepare the tortelli following the instructions for tortellini on page 5 but make the tortelli twice as large (these "tortelli" are really very large tortellini). • Tomato Sauce: Heat the oil in a medium saucepan with the bay leaves, basil, garlic, thyme, and orange zest. • Add the tomatoes and season with salt. Simmer over medium heat until reduced a little, 10–15 minutes. • Add the orange juice and cook for 1 minute. Remove from the heat and press through a strainer. • Cook the pasta in batches in a large pot of salted boiling water until al dente, 3–4 minutes. • Use a slotted spoon to transfer to serving dishes. • Serve hot with the sauce, topped with the reserved asparagus.

1 quantity Plain Pasta Dough
(see page 4)

Filling

12 oz (350 g) asparagus,
cut into short lengths
12 oz (350 g) boiling potatoes
1 clove garlic, finely chopped
1/4 cup (60 g) butter
1 tablespoon onion seeds
Salt and freshly ground white pepper

Tomato Sauce

1/4 cup (60 ml) extra-virgin olive oil
2 bay leaves
4 leaves basil, torn
2 cloves garlic, finely chopped
1 tablespoon finely chopped fresh thyme
Finely grated zest and freshly squeezed
juice of 1 orange
1 1/2 lb (750 g) firm-ripe tomatoes,
peeled, seeded, and chopped
Salt

SERVES 4–6

PREPARATION 1 h + time for pasta

COOKING 1 h

DIFFICULTY level 3

Artichoke Ravioli

Prepare the pasta dough and set aside to rest. • Clean the artichokes and chop coarsely. Place in a bowl of cold water with the lemon juice. • Melt the butter in a medium saucepan and sweat the scallion with a pinch of salt over low heat for 10 minutes. • Drain the artichokes and add to the pan along with the walnuts. Season with salt and pepper. Cover and cook over low heat for 40 minutes, adding the milk gradually. • Chop the filling in a food processor. Transfer to a bowl and mix in the Parmesan, egg, and enough of the bread crumbs to obtain a firm mixture. • Divide the pasta dough into 4 pieces. • Roll out the pasta and prepare the ravioli as shown on page 5. • Place the ravioli on a lightly floured cloth until ready to cook. • Cook the pasta in a large pot of salted boiling water until al dente, 3–4 minutes. • Use a slotted spoon to transfer to serving dishes. • Drizzle with the butter and sprinkle with the Parmesan. • Serve hot.

1 quantity Plain Pasta Dough
(see page 4)

4 artichokes
Freshly squeezed juice of 1 lemon
2 tablespoons butter
1 scallion (spring onion), finely chopped
Salt and freshly ground white pepper
10 walnuts, shelled and coarsely
chopped
1/4 cup (60 ml) milk
6 tablespoons freshly grated Parmesan
cheese
1 large egg
1/2 cup (75 g) fine dry bread crumbs
1/2 cup (125 g) melted butter
4 tablespoons freshly grated Parmesan
cheese

SERVES 4–6

PREPARATION 45 min + time for pasta

COOKING 35 min

DIFFICULTY level 2

Potato Ravioli
with pesto

Prepare the pasta dough and set aside to rest. • Pesto: Place the basil, pine nuts, garlic, oil, salt, and pepper in a food processor and chop until smooth. • Transfer the mixture to a medium bowl and stir in the cheese and water. • Filling: Boil the potatoes in a large pot of salted boiling water until tender, 15–20 minutes. • Drain and mash in a large bowl. • Bring the wine and water to a boil in a small saucepan. • Add the sausage meat and simmer for about 5 minutes to remove the fat. • Drain, discarding the liquid, and add the sausage meat to the potatoes. Mix in the flour, milk, Parmesan, eggs, and marjoram. If the filling is too sticky, add a little more flour. • Roll out the pasta and prepare the ravioli as shown on page 5. • Cook the pasta in small batches in a large pot of salted boiling water until al dente, 3–4 minutes. • Use a slotted spoon to drain the pasta and place in individual serving dishes. Spoon the pesto over the top. • Serve hot.

1 quantity Plain Pasta Dough
(see page 4)

Pesto
2 cups (45 g) fresh basil leaves
2 tablespoons pine nuts
2 cloves garlic
1/2 cup (125 ml) extra-virgin olive oil
Salt and freshly ground black pepper
4 tablespoons freshly grated Parmesan
2 tablespoons boiling water

Filling
2 lb (1 kg) potatoes, peeled
1/2 cup (125 ml) dry white wine
1 cup (250 ml) water
5 oz (150 g) sausage meat
1/3 cup (50 g) all-purpose (plain) flour
1/2 cup (125 ml) milk
2 tablespoons freshly grated Parmesan
3 large eggs
1/2 teaspoon dried marjoram

Ravioli
with spinach and tomato sauce

Prepare the pasta dough and set aside to rest. • Cook the spinach in salted water until tender, 5–7 minutes. • Drain, squeeze out excess moisture, and chop finely. • Mix the spinach, ricotta, eggs and egg yolk, Parmesan, nutmeg, salt, and pepper in a large bowl. • Roll out the dough and prepare the ravioli as shown on page 5. If preferred, cut out 5-inch (12-cm) squares of pasta dough, place a spoonful of filling in the center, and fold the pasta around it—as shown in the photograph of the finished dish below. • Cook in batches in a large pot of salted boiling water for 4–5 minutes. • Use a slotted spoon to transfer to serving dishes. Serve hot with the sauce.

1 quantity Plain Pasta Dough
(see page 4)

2 lb (1 kg) spinach leaves
2 cups (500 g) fresh ricotta, drained
2 large eggs + 1 large egg yolk
1¼ cups (150 g) freshly grated
Parmesan cheese
Pinch of freshly grated nutmeg
Salt and freshly ground black pepper
1 quantity Tomato Sauce
(see page 8)

Pansôti

with walnut sauce

Prepare the pasta dough and set aside to rest. • Filling: Blanch the greens in salted boiling water for 5 minutes. Drain, squeezing out excess moisture, and coarsely chop. • Mix with the greens, egg, Parmesan, and marjoram in a large bowl. Season with salt and pepper. • Roll out the dough on a lightly floured surface until paper-thin. • Cut into pansôti—triangular shapes of about 1½ inches (4 cm) on each side, or circles about 3 inches (7 cm) in diameter. • Drop small heaps of filling onto the center of each piece of pasta and seal by folding over. • Walnut Sauce: Chop the walnuts, bread crumbs, garlic, and salt in a food processor until creamy. • Mix in the ricotta. • Cook the pasta in small batches in a large pot of salted boiling water until al dente, 3–4 minutes. • Drain and serve hot with the sauce.

1 quantity Plain Pasta Dough (see page 4)

Filling

10 oz (300 g) wild greens, such as dandelion greens, beet greens, wild chicory, borage, burnet, wild greens, or cress

1 cup (250 g) ricotta, drained

1 large egg, lightly beaten

¼ cup (30 g) freshly grated Parmesan cheese

1 tablespoon finely chopped fresh marjoram

Salt and freshly ground black pepper

Walnut Sauce

½ cup (60 g) walnuts

2 tablespoons fresh bread crumbs, soaked in milk and squeezed dry

4 cloves garlic

Salt

½ cup (120 g) ricotta cheese, drained

SERVES 4

PREPARATION 30 min + time for pasta

COOKING 15 min

DIFFICULTY level 3

Zucchini Ravioli

with butter and rosemary

Prepare the pasta dough and set aside to rest. • Cook the zucchini in a pot of salted, boiling water until tender. Drain, place in a bowl, and mash with a fork. Add the amaretti, ricotta, two-thirds of the Parmesan, and nutmeg. Season with salt. Mix well to form a thick cream. If the filling is too liquid, add dry bread crumbs. • Roll out the pasta and prepare the ravioli as shown on page 5. • Cook the ravioli in a large pot of salted boiling water until al dente, 3–4 minutes. Drain well and place in a heated serving dish. • Sauce: Place the garlic in a small saucepan with the butter and rosemary and simmer for 1–2 minutes over medium heat, stirring frequently. • Pour the sauce over the ravioli, sprinkle with the remaining Parmesan, and serve hot.

1 quantity Plain Pasta Dough (see page 4)

Filling
2 medium zucchini (courgettes)
1 cup (150 g) crushed amaretti cookies
$^2/_3$ cup (150 g) fresh ricotta cheese
1 cup (120 g) freshly grated Parmesan cheese
$^1/_4$ teaspoon nutmeg
Salt
$^1/_2$ cup (75 g) fine dry bread crumbs

Sauce
1 clove garlic, finely chopped
$^1/_2$ cup (125 g) butter
2 tablespoons finely chopped fresh rosemary

48

Fish Ravioli
with vegetable sauce

Prepare the pasta dough and set aside to rest. • Filling: Melt the butter in a large frying pan. Add the fish and cook over medium heat until tender, about 5 minutes. Chop the fish very finely. • Cook the Swiss chard in a pot of salted water until tender, 5–7 minutes. Squeeze out excess moisture and chop finely. • Combine the fish and chard in a bowl with the ricotta, eggs, half the Parmesan, and nutmeg. Season with salt and mix well. • Roll out the pasta and prepare the ravioli as shown on page 5. • Sauce: Put the mushrooms in a small bowl of warm water and soak for 15 minutes. • Drain well and chop finely. • Put the celery, onion, parsley, and butter in the pan used to cook the fish. Add the tomatoes and water, and simmer over low heat for 20 minutes. Season with salt and add the pine nuts. • Cook the ravioli in a large pot of salted boiling until al dente, 3–4 minutes. Drain and place in a heated serving dish. • Pour the sauce over the top, sprinkle with the remaining Parmesan, and serve hot.

1 quantity Plain Pasta Dough
  (see page 4)

Filling
1/4 cup (60 g) butter
14 oz (400 g) firm white fish fillets
12 oz (350 g) fresh Swiss chard
  (silverbeet)
2 oz (60 g) fresh ricotta cheese
2 large eggs
1 cup (120 g) freshly grated Parmesan
  cheese
1/4 teaspoon nutmeg
Salt

Sauce
2 tablespoons dried mushrooms
1 stalk celery, 1 onion, 1 tablespoon
  parsley, all finely chopped
1/2 cup (125 g) butter
4 ripe tomatoes, peeled and chopped
1 cup (250 ml) water
1/4 cup (30 g) pine nuts, toasted and
  finely chopped

SERVES 4–6

PREPARATION 30 min + time for pasta

COOKING 15 min

DIFFICULTY level 3

Potato Tortelli
with butter and parmesan

Prepare the pasta dough and set aside to rest. • Boil the potatoes in a large pan of lightly salted water until tender. Drain well and slip off the skins. Mash until smooth. • Sauté the pancetta, onion, and garlic in a large frying pan over medium heat until pale golden brown, about 5 minutes. • Season generously with pepper and add to the potatoes. • Stir in the ricotta and Parmesan and season with salt, pepper, and nutmeg. Set aside to cool completely. • Roll out the pasta and prepare the tortelli as shown on page 5. • Cook the tortelli in batches until al dente, 3–4 minutes. • Remove with a slotted spoon. • Serve hot with melted butter and plenty of freshly grated Parmesan cheese.

1 quantity Plain Pasta Dough
(see page 4)

Filling
2 lb (1 kg) potatoes
3 oz (90 g) pancetta, finely chopped
1 medium white onion, finely chopped
2 cloves garlic, finely chopped
5 oz (150 g) ricotta cheese, drained
$\frac{1}{2}$ cup (60 g) freshly grated Parmesan
cheese
Freshly grated nutmeg
Salt and freshly ground black pepper

Melted butter and freshly grated
Parmesan cheese, to serve

SERVES 4

PREPARATION 25 min + time for pasta

COOKING 10 min

DIFFICULTY level 3

Tortellini
with truffles

Prepare the pasta dough and set aside to rest. • Filling: Heat the butter in a large frying pan and sauté the pork and chicken over medium heat for about 5 minutes. Remove from the pan and chop finely in a food processor. • Sauté the prosciutto and mortadella in the same pan for 2–3 minutes. • Combine the pork, chicken, prosciutto, and mortadella in a bowl. Add the eggs, ½ cup (60 g) of Parmesan, nutmeg, salt, and pepper. Mix well and set aside. • Prepare the tortellini following the instructions on page 5. • Cook the tortellini in a large pot of salted boiling water until al dente, 3–4 minutes. • Sauce: Melt the butter in a saucepan over low heat. Stir in the cream and simmer for 2–3 minutes. • When the tortellini are cooked, drain well and place in the pan with the cream. Add the remaining Parmesan, the truffle, salt, and pepper, and toss gently over medium-low heat for 1–2 minutes. Serve hot.

1 quantity Plain Pasta Dough
(see page 4)

Filling
2 tablespoons butter
2 oz (60 g) lean pork,
coarsely chopped
2 oz (60 g) chicken breast,
coarsely chopped
2 oz (60 g) prosciutto (Parma ham),
finely chopped
4 oz (125 g) mortadella,
finely chopped
2 large eggs
¾ cup (90 g) freshly grated Parmesan
cheese
¼ teaspoon nutmeg
Salt and freshly ground black pepper

Sauce
⅓ cup (90 g) butter
½ cup (125 ml) heavy (double) cream
1 small truffle, white or black,
in shavings

SERVES 4–6

PREPARATION 15 min + time for pasta

COOKING 20 min

DIFFICULTY level 3

Tortellini
Bologna style

Prepare the pasta dough and set aside to rest. • Dry-fry the pork in a nonstick frying pan. Begin cooking over high heat, then turn once to seal. Reduce the heat and cook for 4–5 minutes until cooked through. Remove from heat and season with salt. • Chop the pork with the mortadella and prosciutto in a food processor until finely ground. • Add half the egg (reserve the rest for another use) and Parmesan. Season with salt, pepper, and nutmeg. Transfer to a bowl and refrigerate for 2 hours. • Form into ½-inch (1-cm) balls and set aside. • Prepare the tortellini following the instructions on page 5. • Cook the pasta in the boiling stock until al dente, 3–4 minutes. Ladle into heated serving bowls and serve hot.

1 quantity Plain Pasta Dough
(see page 4)

Filling
4 oz (150 g) lean pork,
cut in small cubes
Salt
4 oz (125 g) mortadella
4 oz (125 g) prosciutto (Parma ham)
1 large egg, lightly beaten
3 tablespoons freshly grated Parmesan
cheese
Freshly ground black pepper
$\frac{1}{8}$ teaspoon freshly grated nutmeg
$2\frac{1}{2}$ quarts (2.5 liters) beef stock
(homemade or bouillon cube)

SERVES 4–6

PREPARATION 1 h + time for pasta

COOKING 45 min

DIFFICULTY level 3

Baked Ravioli
with tomato sauce

Prepare the pasta dough and set aside to rest. • Filling: Boil the spinach in lightly salted water until tender, 5–7 minutes. Drain well, squeeze dry, and chop finely. • Sauté the spinach in the butter in a medium frying pan over medium heat for 2 minutes. Season with salt, pepper, and nutmeg and sprinkle with the flour. • Pour in the milk and simmer over low heat until the mixture is moist but no liquid remains, about 5 minutes. • Remove from the heat and let cool. Mix in the egg yolk and Parmesan. • Roll out the pasta and prepare the ravioli as shown on page 5. • Preheat the oven to 400°F (200°C/gas 6). • Butter a baking dish. • Cook the pasta in small batches in a large pot of salted boiling water until al dente, 3–4 minutes. • Use a slotted spoon to transfer to the prepared baking dish, filling the dish in layers with the ravioli, melted butter, tomato sauce, and the Parmesan. • Bake for 12–15 minutes, or until the cheese is bubbling. • Serve hot.

1 quantity Plain Pasta Dough (see page 4)

Filling
2½ cups (600 g) spinach leaves
¼ cup (60 g) butter
Salt and freshly ground white pepper
⅛ teaspoon freshly grated nutmeg
1 tablespoon all-purpose (plain) flour
¼ cup (60 ml) milk
1 large egg yolk
½ cup (60 g) freshly grated Parmesan cheese

To Serve
⅓ cup (90 g) butter, melted
¾ cup (180 ml unseasoned tomato sauce, storebought or homemade
1 cup (125 g) freshly grated Parmesan cheese

Baked Crêpes

Crêpes: Mix the flour and salt in a medium bowl. • Add the eggs, beating until just blended. • Pour in the milk and use a balloon whisk to beat until smooth. Let rest in a cool place for 1 hour. • Preheat the oven to 400°F (200°C/gas 6). • Set out a baking dish. • Filling: Mix the ricotta, Parmesan, mozzarella, parsley, and basil in a large bowl. Season with salt and pepper. • Heat a small amount of the oil in a crêpe pan or small frying pan over medium heat. Stir the batter and pour in about 2 tablespoons, tilting the pan so the batter forms a thin, even layer. Cook until the top is set and the bottom is golden, about 1 minute. Turn the crêpe over and cook until lightly browned, about 30 seconds. Repeat, oiling the pan each time, until all the batter is used. Stack the crêpes between sheets of parchment paper. • Spread evenly with the filling, roll up, and arrange, seam side down, in the baking dish. Cover with the tomato sauce and sprinkle with Parmesan. • Bake for 12–15 minutes, or until the cheese is golden brown. • Serve hot.

Crêpes
2/3 cup (100 g) all-purpose (plain) flour
1/8 teaspoon salt
4 large eggs
1 cup (250 ml) milk
2 tablespoons extra-virgin olive oil

Filling
1 1/4 cups (300 g) ricotta cheese
1/4 cup (30 g) freshly grated Parmesan cheese
8 oz (250 g) fresh mozzarella, cut into small cubes

1 tablespoon finely chopped fresh parsley
4–6 leaves fresh basil, torn
Salt and freshly ground white pepper
1 cup (250 ml) storebought unseasoned tomato sauce
1/4 cup (30 g) freshly grated Parmesan cheese

Sweet Ravioli

Pasta Dough: Combine the flour and salt in a mound on a work surface and make a well in the center. Break the eggs into the well and mix in to form a stiff dough. Knead for 15–20 minutes, until smooth and elastic. • Press the dough into a disk, wrap in plastic wrap (cling film), and let rest for 30 minutes. • Ricotta Filling: Mix the ricotta, egg, egg yolk, sugar, and cinnamon in a large bowl. • Roll out the dough on a lightly floured work surface until very thin. Cut into 8-inch (20-cm) long strips and arrange pellets of filling near one edge about ¾ inch (2 cm) apart. Fold each strip of dough lengthwise to cover the filling. Seal, then cut into squares with a fluted pastry cutter. • Heat the oil in a large frying pan until very hot. Fry the ravioli in small batches until golden brown. • Drain on paper towels. • Dust with confectioners' sugar and serve hot.

Pasta Dough
1⅓ cups (200 g) all-purpose (plain) flour
¼ teaspoon salt
2 large eggs

Ricotta Filling
1¾ cups (450 g) ricotta cheese, drained
1 large egg + 1 large egg yolk, beaten
1 tablespoon sugar
¼ teaspoon ground cinnamon

4 cups (1 liter) peanut oil, for frying
½ cup (75 g) confectioners' sugar, to dust

SERVES 4–6

PREPARATION 30 min + time for pasta

COOKING 40 min

DIFFICULTY level 3

Spinach Roll

Prepare the pasta dough and set aside to rest. • Finely chop the spinach and sauté in 7 tablespoons of butter in a large frying pan over medium heat for 2 minutes. • Remove from the heat and let cool completely. • Drain the Ricotta in a fine mesh strainer and mix it in with ¾ cup (90 g) of Parmesan. Season with salt and pepper. • Use a large rubber spatula to spread the mixture over the pasta rectangle, leaving a small border at the edges. • Roll up and wrap the dough in a clean kitchen cloth. Tie each end with kitchen string and tie the roll in the center. • Bring a long saucepan (a fish poacher is ideal) filled with salted water to the boil. Lower the pasta roll into it and cook over low heat for 30 minutes. • Remove from the water and remove from the cloth. • Slice the pasta roll ½-inch (1-cm) thick and arrange on serving plates. • Melt the remaining tablespoon of butter with the sage in a small saucepan. Discard the sage. Pour over the slices and sprinkle with the remaining Parmesan.

1 quantity Plain Pasta Dough
  (see page 4)

2 cups (500 g) cooked, drained spinach
½ cup (125 g) butter, melted
1¼ cups (310 g) ricotta cheese
1 cup (125 g) freshly grated Parmesan
  cheese
Salt and freshly ground white pepper
1 small bunch fresh sage

Index

Filled Pasta

was created and produced by McRae Books Srl

Via del Salviatino 1 – 50016 Fiesole, (Florence) Italy

info@mcraebooks.com

Publishers: Anne McRae and Marco Nardi

Project Director: Anne McRae

Design: Sara Mathews

Text: McRae Books archive

Editing: Carla Bardi

Photography: Studio Lanza (Lorenzo Borri, Cristina Canepari, Ke-ho Casati, Mauro Corsi, Gil Gallo, Leonardo Pasquinelli, Gianni Petronio, Stefano Pratesi, Sandra Preussinger)

Home Economist: Benedetto Rillo

Artbuying: McRae Books

Layouts: Aurora Granata, Filippo Delle Monache, Davide Gasparri

Repro: Fotolito Raf, Florence

ISBN 978-88-6098-077-9

Printed and bound in China